THE MAKING OF DOG

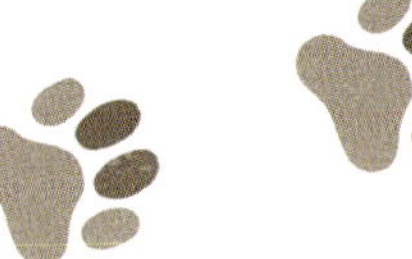

PRIYA SAWHNEY

Illustrated by
Sumedha Sah

tota books

THE MAKING OF DOG

Published by arrangement with the author
Illustrations by Sumedha Sah

First Indian Paperback Edition, 2014

ISBN 978-81-7621-262-5

Published by
tota books
An imprint of **FULL CIRCLE** *PUBLISHING*
J-40, Jorbagh Lane, New Delhi-110003
Tel: 011-24620063, 24621011
Fax: 24645795
contact@fullcirclebooks.in
www.fullcirclebooks.in

Design and layout: Sumedha Sah

Printed at J.J. Imprints Pvt. Ltd., A-24, Sector-68, Noida-201301 (U.P.)

PRINTED IN INDIA

14/14/03/01/10/SS/JJI/JJI/NP250/NP250

For Ahanaa and Anavi Puri and the Puri parents, with love.
As also for Usha Kapur, Dipika Sawhney Nanjappa and Arun Kapur.
For Charlotte Avebäck, love and thanks for the encouragement and editing.
For Niklas Henricson – with hopes that this one will get read faster than the other.
And for Lennart Sjöström, Hero of Heroes and best friend. Words will never be enough.

First God made the world. He made the sea and the fish that darted everywhere. And the land with the emerald green forests and the butterflies and the silver birch and the deer and the giraffe, lions and panthers.

And horses. And birds of every kind, from the demure sparrow to the sparkling kingfisher. And flowers. So many flowers. Daffodils, roses, geraniums, sunflowers, little wildflowers...

And then he made man.

But he needed something really really wonderful, something... someone...amazing. Fantabulous.

Superduperexcitinghappyabulous!!

What, what, what?

He sat down and thought.

Okay, okay, God is everywhere. So he doesn't have a seat, really. Just think of a mind, spread all over the world, laying quiet for a minute and bringing all its power to bear on a really wonderful, wonderful creation.

WHAT, WHAT, WHAT could it be!...

"May I venture a suggestion?" asked the hippopotamous, strolling by. God, courteous and polite as he always is, answered, "certainly".

Something Fantasticous!
Something Triumphicous!
Something Gigantiwonderous!

"In short," the hippopotamous said, clearing his throat and trying to look modest, even if it was hard... "In short, something just like me"

"Harrumph!"

snorted the elephant, who had followed the hippopotamus to make sure that he was not, ONCE AGAIN, going to ask God to give him a trunk longer than the elephant's. "Gigantiwonderous indeed. Do you not see that God has already made the most wonderful thing in the world? What could be more gigantic and wondrous than me?"

SPLASH!

The elephant had his answer as the blue whale's huge splash in the distance sent ripples across the water in all directions.

"Not now, children," God's gentle voice always had the power to soothe, filled as it was with love for all his creations, "I'm thinking".

And indeed, he was thinking, in all the many forms that he had. After all, the Christian God and the Hindu Gods and Allah, and all of the Gods are one.

And no matter who you pray to, God will always listen if the prayer is with a good heart and you really mean it.

“He’s thinking,” “God’s thinking,” “Shhh, God’s thinking,” the whispers spread quickly across the planet.

The waves hushed their rolling song, the eagles soaring high above in the sky dived and wheeled as gently as they could, feather-soft in the empty skies (remember, this was before man started filling the sky with aeroplanes and balloons and rockets) and even the wind stood still.

The whole earth took a deep breath and held it, and in the hush that followed God's mind could clearly be heard thinking. It sounded like the leaves in the forest on a summer's day, when the sun is shining and the wildflowers are in full bloom.

Like the stars on a snowy night, when it's all white and it's only you standing there breathing in the crisp cool air. Like the sea at sunset, with the glow of the setting sun rippling across the gently rolling waves...you get my point.

And so the world held its breath. And God thought. And thought. And thought.

No one had ever seen him think this long. "Mummy," whispered the little angelfish behind a rock in the big lake "if he is thinking so long, what if the creature he makes is someone he loves more than us?"

"Hush now," the mother angelfish's fins swished gently. "God loves everyone the same."

"Indeed I do." The words were just a thought, from the omnipresent mind of God, a gentle murmur wrapping itself around the baby angelfish and spreading from there like a blanket of love over the whole planet. "I love you all, always."

"But then why do you need to make something more wonderful than me?" asked the elephant, somewhat softly because he had just dried off and didn't want the blue whale to hear him.

“Oh my dear little ones!” God replied kindly (and only God would dare refer to the elephant and blue whales as little ones, you and me should never try to do that). “I didn’t mean to make something more wonderful than you! You’re each of you so wonderful already. Look at you, with your big ears and useful trunk! And you – the biggest and smallest of fish in your grace and beauty as you frolic underwater! And the skies at dawn and dusk. And the cheetah, speedy and swift! The black panther...the flowers... And look at each leaf on every tree, just look!!! Every living being is already wonderful,” God explained.

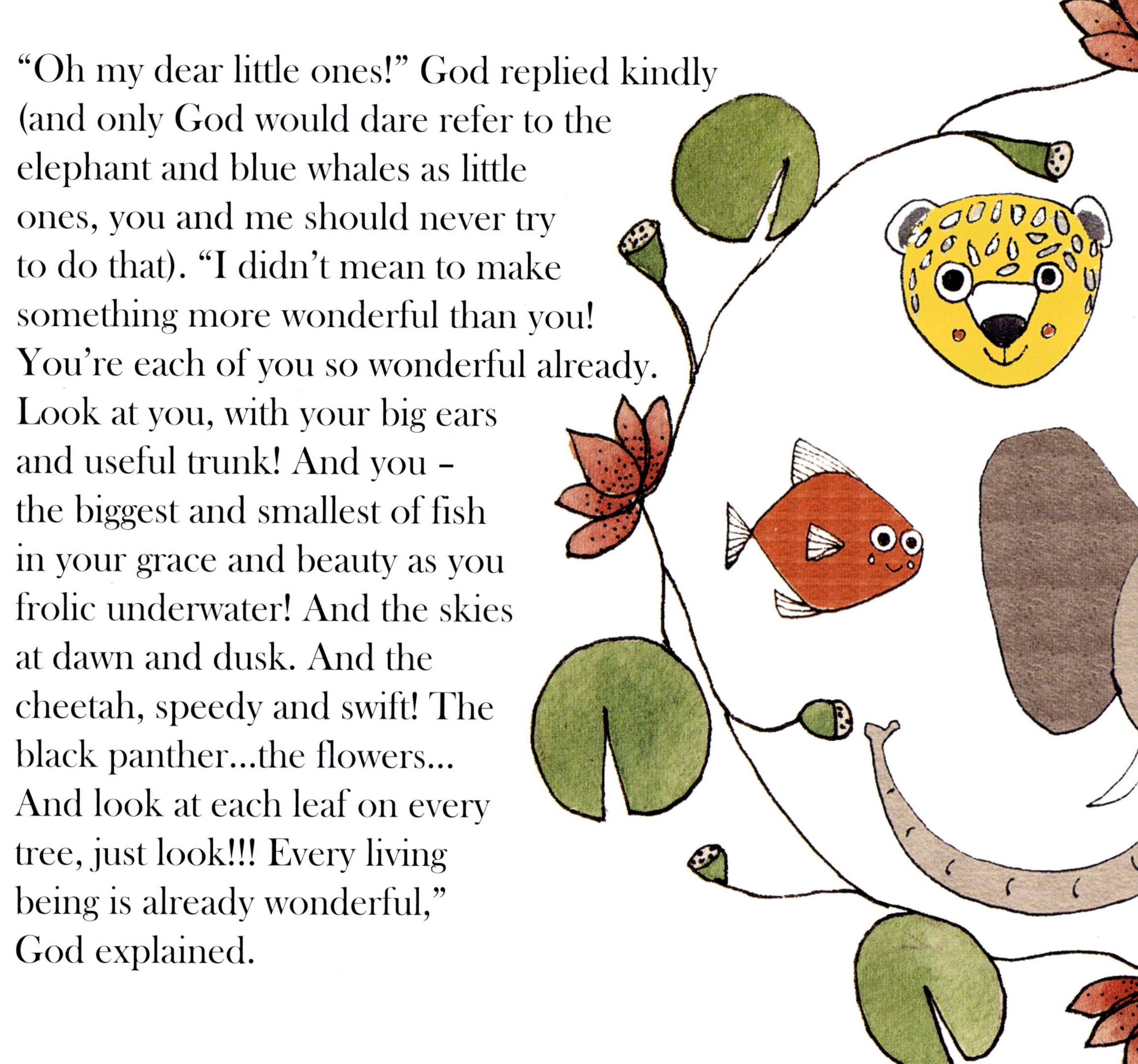

"But there will come times when my human creations will need help and a reminder of how wonderful life is. They'll need someone to love them no matter what, someone who can make them laugh, someone who'll bring out the best in them..." God's voice trailed off as he looked at the expectant beings around him. Horse, with his warm chestnut mane. Lion, brave and proud. Slightly wet elephant, listening and memorising as only an elephant can. In the distance the dolphins playing games... and an idea came to God.

And this is how Dog came to be.

Furry and warm like horse, but smaller so they could be easier to cuddle. Brave and courageous like lion, and loyal and ever-remembering like elephants. Playful as dolphins and trusting as the baby angelfish.

And above all, full of love and forgiveness. Dog is, after all, even in name just a reflection of God. And that meant Dog had to be blessed with unconditional love, to be there for humans and others and to give humans the chance to give unconditional love in return.

WOOF!

And that is how Dog was made.

Priya Sawhney lives in Sweden. Born in India, as a child she dreamed of being a vet and rescuing all the animals in the world. Although she didn't get to become a vet she has succeeded in helping rescue many many animals, mainly dogs – and her own dog is also rescued from the streets in Stockholm. Priya is also a volunteer with WSPA (the World Society for Protection of Animals) and her favourite people are vets and animal rescuers. Priya also works with telecommunications as part of her daily life.